Most Influential Hip-Hop Artists

Andrea Cameron • Marcella Runell Hall

Series Editor
Jeffrey D. Wilhelm

Much thought, debate, and research went into choosing and ranking the 10 items in each book in this series. We realize that everyone has his or her own opinion of what is most significant, revolutionary, amazing, deadly, and so on. As you read, you may agree with our choices, or you may be surprised — and that's the way it should be!

Franklin Watts
an imprint of
SCHOLASTIC
www.scholastic.com/librarypublishing

A Rubicon book published in association with Scholastic Inc.

Ru'bĭcon © 2008 Rubicon Publishing Inc.
www.rubiconpublishing.com

Associate Publishers: Kim Koh, Miriam Bardswich
Project Editor: Amy Land
Editor: Christine Boocock
Creative Director: Jennifer Drew
Project Manager/Designer: Jeanette MacLean
Graphic Designer: Samara Parent

The publisher gratefully acknowledges the following for permission to reprint copyrighted material in this book.

Every reasonable effort has been made to trace the owners of copyrighted material and to make due acknowledgment. Any errors or omissions drawn to our attention will be gladly rectified in future editions.

"Unlikely Star" (excerpt) from "Death to Eminem: Long Live Marshall Mathers" by Matthew McKinnon, July 26, 2005. Source: CBC.ca. Permission courtesy of CBC.ca.

Cover image: Run-DMC–© Kevin Knight/Corbis

Library and Archives Canada Cataloguing in Publication

Hall, Marcella Runell
        The 10 most influential hip hop artists / Marcella Runell Hall and Andrea Cameron.

Includes index.
ISBN: 978-1-55448-504-8

        1. Readers (Elementary). 2. Readers—Hip-hop. I. Cameron, Andrea II. Title. III. Title: Ten most influential hip-hop artists.

PE1117.H34 2007   428.6   C2007-906920-7

1 2 3 4 5 6 7 8 9 10   10   17 16 15 14 13 12 11 10 09 08

Printed in Singapore

Contents

6

14

30

HIP-HOP NATION

When you think hip hop, what comes to mind? Do you think of the extravagant lifestyle of some of today's hottest hip-hop stars? Do you think of the inner city, the place where hip-hop started? Or do you think of the message that hip-hop artists are trying to get across through their music? Perhaps all of these things come to mind. One of the fascinating things about hip hop is that it involves such diverse ideas and beliefs. Another fascinating thing is how it has affected pop culture — everything from fashion to movies, and the English language.

Since the birth of rock and roll, no musical style has revolutionized popular music and culture as much as hip hop. An urban genre, it was born on big city streets. As the genre's popularity grew, people embraced it as a way to give a voice to the oppressed. Hip hop went on to rise above race, class, religion, language, and nationality.

In this book, we feature the 10 most influential hip-hop artists. In choosing and ranking them, we considered the following criteria: Were the artist's music and look innovative? Whether rhyming about poverty, feminism, racism, or spirituality, was the artist's message strong? We also measured each artist's success — how much recognition did each one get for his or her songs? Finally, we looked at each artist's influence on future performers.

The people on this list have all done something unique. Discover how each one helped to popularize an art form that many thought was just a fad.

---

genre: *style or category of music*
oppressed: *those who are mistreated or kept down by unjust forces*

WHO IS THE MOST INFLUENTIAL HIP-HOP ARTIST?

10 BIG PUN

Big Pun died in November 2000 from obesity-related health issues. It is estimated that he weighed more than 695 pounds at the time.

Take some clever wordplay, a Latin vibe, and a talent for tongue-twisting rhymes and what do you get? A Latin hip-hop star named Big Pun.

Big Pun was born in the South Bronx on November 10, 1971. Big Pun grew up at the center of it all — hip hop was also born in the South Bronx during the early 1970s. By the time Big Pun was a teenager, he knew he wanted to be a part of hip-hop culture. His first solo album shot him and Latin hip hop into the spotlight! *Capital Punishment* was a huge hit. The album "mixed hints of salsa and a few Spanish lyrics with smooth rhythm-and-blues tracks and stark New York hip hop," according to *New York Times* music critic Jon Pareles. The album eventually sold more than two million copies! "Latin hip hop really showed its strength and staying power when ... Big Pun became the first Latino to go platinum," according to *Latin Beat* writer Melissa Castillo-Garstow.

Big Pun followed his double platinum debut with 2000's *Yeeeah Baby*. Sadly, he didn't live to see it become a success. Big Pun died in 2000 at the age of 28. Despite his early death, Big Pun made big strides for Latin rappers in the hip-hop scene.

BIG PUN

Big Pun had a pretty tough childhood. In what ways do you think this influenced his music later in life?

EARLY DAYS

Growing up, Big Pun witnessed his mother's problems with substance abuse. He also had to deal with his father leaving the family. When Big Pun was 15 years old, he dropped out of high school. He also left home. It was during this time that Big Pun started writing rhymes and performing with other artists. His "imaginative lyrics and smooth delivery," soon got him noticed according to the *New York Times*. In his own words, Big Pun rapped "about everyday life, losing your job, losing a loved one, stress, happiness, whatever."

BIG BREAK

In 1995, Big Pun met fellow Puerto Rican rapper Fat Joe. By this time, Fat Joe had already released a successful album called *Represent*. Fat Joe hired Big Pun to perform on his 1995 album, *Jealous One's Envy*. In the late 1990s, "Latinos were the hottest trend," according to Raquel Rivera, author of *New York Ricans from the Hip Hop Zone*. The success of Big Pun's 1998 album, *Capital Punishment,* made him part of the craze! As she writes, "Suddenly, in '98 and '99, Big Pun [became] the hottest thing and [was] on every track and video." Fans immediately noticed Pun's talent for wordplay. His complex, meaningful lyrics and rhymes challenged listeners.

AT THE TOP

On the song "Glamour Life" from *Capital Punishment*, Pun rapped that he was "A living legend from the Bronx, second to none, unless it's Pun." In 1999, he was nominated for a Grammy Award for Best Rap Album for *Capital Punishment*. He was the first Latin rapper ever nominated for a Grammy! His success helped open doors for other Latin hip-hop artists. Big Pun's second album, *Yeeeah Baby*, was released shortly after his death. According to music critic John Bush, Big Pun "salute[d] his Latin heritage all over the album, switching from street slang to Latin lingo without batting an eye." This album sold over 500,000 copies within three months.

Big Pun at the 41st Annual Grammy Awards in 1999

During his career, Big Pun performed on albums for everyone from J.Lo to Fat Joe! Do you think it's good for artists to become famous performing on other people's albums? Or do you think artists have more success when they focus on their solo careers? Explain.

Quick Fact

After Big Pun's death, his wife, Liza Rios, set up the Big Pun Foundation in his memory. According to Rios, "My husband wanted his success to serve as an inspiration for youth in urban communities."

10   **9**   **8**   **7**   **6**

IN MEMORIAM

Big Pun had a big impact on hip hop. Read these quotations to find out what some industry heavyweights had to say about Big Pun after his death.

"Big Pun, like any rare talent, was a true original in the art of rap. ... Pun's lyrical fire burned bright behind what others saw as a laid-back demeanor."

— **Asia Song, *Car Audio* magazine**

lyrical: *poetic; deeply emotional*
demeanor: *behavior; outward manner*

"[Big Pun] was a legend. Not only to Latinos but hip hop in general. He broke many barriers. I think he was the birth of that 'Latino explosion.'"

— **Fat Joe, rapper and Big Pun's producer and manager**

producer: *music industry professional who invents beats and polishes an artist's sound*

"Big Pun's second album *Yeeeah Baby* proves the rapper's demise was doubly tragic. ... *Yeeeah Baby* displays an artist evolving beyond his previous work with remarkable ease."

— **John Bush, allmusic.com**

demise: *death*
evolving: *growing; developing gradually*

"The trademark of his style was to take a deep breath and pour out rhyme after quick-talking rhyme."

— **Jon Pareles, *The New York Times***

"Bronx rapper Big Pun (born Christopher Rios) is widely acknowledged to be one of the most gifted MCs ever to breathe life into a microphone."

— **Nathan Brackett, *The New Rolling Stone Album Guide***

MCs: *short for masters of ceremonies; microphone controllers*

The Expert Says...

Pun attacked standard hip-hop topics with witty, unpredictable elasticity.

— Matt Diehl, *Rolling Stone* magazine

elasticity: *flexibility*

Take Note

Big Pun is our pick for #10. This talented rapper opened the door for Latino artists in the hip-hop scene. He was also the most successful Latino rapper of his day — the first to be nominated for a Grammy! Big Pun achieved all of this by the time he was 28. Had he lived longer, who knows what Big Pun might have been able to accomplish?

• Big Pun's three kids are following their father down the hip-hop path. In what ways do you think their father's early death and great success might influence them?

9 SALT-N-PEPA

Hip-hop stars (from left) Sandy Denton, Cheryl James, and Deidra Roper at the VH1 Hip Hop Honors Award Show in 2006.

ALSO KNOWN AS: Cheryl "Salt" James, Sandra "Pepa" Denton, and Deidra "DJ Spinderella" Roper are the three women who shot to fame as Salt-n-Pepa.

SLAMMIN' STYLE! Salt-n-Pepa was the first all-female rap group to make an impact on the male-dominated hip-hop scene.

From the first time Salt-n-Pepa performed, the group stood out from the crowd. This was one of the first all-female hip-hop groups to make it big. Salt-n-Pepa was also one of the first rap groups to cross into the pop mainstream. The group helped establish hip hop's widespread acceptance in the late 1980s.

When they first met while working at Sears, Cheryl James and Sandra Denton probably didn't think they had a future in hip hop. But by the end of 1985, the two were performing at local clubs under the name Super Nature. In 1986, Super Nature became Salt-n-Pepa and released its debut album, *Hot, Cool and Vicious*. The album's opening track, a dance song called "Push It," was "one of the first rap songs to hit number one on the dance singles charts," according to music critic Steve Huey. The song, "about pushing it on the dance floor" according to Salt, was a huge hit. Plenty of radio play helped the group's popularity rise. The album was the first by an all-female rap group to go platinum!

Thanks to the instant success of "Push It," many critics labeled Salt-n-Pepa a one-hit wonder. Were they ever wrong! During the group's successful career, Salt-n-Pepa earned multiple Grammy nominations and won one Grammy Award. The group also won two MTV Video Music Awards. Salt-n-Pepa's funky sound and bold attitude secured the band's place in hip-hop history!

funky: *jazzy or blues-based music*

SALT-N-PEPA

EARLY DAYS

Cheryl James, a Brooklyn, New York native, and Sandra Denton, an immigrant from Kingston, Jamaica, met in the mid '80s. In 1985, the two teamed up to help a coworker write and perform a song for a class. "The Show Stoppa" became an underground success! The song hit #46 on the Billboard R&B charts. It gave James and Denton the push they needed to switch career paths. The two formed Super Nature along with DJ Pamela Greene. After the group released its first album, Deidra Roper replaced Greene and took the name DJ Spinderella. Together, the three "kicked open the doors for female MCs and DJs in the rap scene," according to VH1.

DJ: *disc jockey; person who spins and scratches records and plays samples in a hip-hop group*

James (left), Roper, and Denton rockin' some '80s styles.

The Expert Says...

" [Salt-n-Pepa] were the first all-female hip-hop group to gain commercial success in a genre dominated by men, opening doors for [other] female hip-hop artists ... "

— Kembrew McLeod, *The St. James Encyclopedia of Pop Culture*

BIG BREAK

Salt-n-Pepa's massive hit, "Push It," was one of the first rap songs to be nominated for a Grammy Award. After a lackluster second album, the group released 1990's *Blacks' Magic*. "This time they worked from a funkier R&B base that brought them more credibility among hip-hop and urban audiences," writes music critic Steve Huey. On the album, the group successfully mixed rap with pop sounds — the group's songs were huge crossover hits! The members of the group became known for their bold, confident, and sassy image.

AT THE TOP

Very Necessary was Salt-n-Pepa's fourth album. Released in 1993, the album was sophisticated and daring. It reflected the group's newfound interest in writing and producing its own music. On the album, the group discussed topics such as femininity, relationships, respect, and love. These topics were "a world apart from those of the gangsta rap that was so popular circa 1993." *Very Necessary* went multi-platinum. It cemented the group's place in hip-hop history.

lackluster: *dull; lacking excitement*
crossover hits: *songs that appeal to fans of various kinds of music*
circa: *around the time of*

 In what ways do you think the women in Salt-n-Pepa portrayed themselves differently than other women in hip hop? Do you think the image they established for themselves improved how women in hip hop are portrayed? Explain.

WHATTA BAND!

Salt-n-Pepa's confidence allowed the group to break into a male-dominated genre. It not only survived, but excelled! The members of this group were innovators and role models in hip-hop culture. Here is a list of the ways this group pushed hip hop's limits!

1) LyRiCs

This group's smart lyrics were in-your-face but humorous at the same time. Salt-n-Pepa's lyrics celebrated femininity and criticized double standards in the industry.

3) FEMiNiSM

Before Salt-n-Pepa made it big, women in hip hop were usually backup singers or dancers. Salt-n-Pepa rejected these roles. The all-female group took responsibility for the whole artistic process. The members of the group were known as performers but they also wrote and produced much of their own material.

double standards: *sets of principles allowing greater opportunities for one than another*

2) GROUNDBREAKING

Salt-n-Pepa showed that women in hip hop didn't have to rely on men for success. The group proved that female hip-hop stars could be strong, positive role models for fans. Artists like Queen Latifah, Missy Elliott, and Lauryn Hill all benefited from Salt-n-Pepa's lead. They have all emphasized their role as intelligent, confident, and independent female artists.

4) LONgEViTy

Salt-n-Pepa had an unusually long career. The group released successful albums in both the 1980s and 1990s. Two members of the group are still in the spotlight with *The Salt-n-Pepa Show*, a reality TV series that debuted in 2007.

Salt-n-Pepa called it quits in 2002. In 2007, Salt and Pepa reunited for The Salt-n-Pepa Show *on VH1.*

? According to Pepa, "Group-wise, there hasn't been another Salt-n-Pepa." Do you agree with her? Explain your point of view.

Quick Fact

In 1994, Salt-n-Pepa finally won a Grammy Award for Best Rap Performance, for their single "None of Your Business." This award made them the first female group to win a Grammy for rap.

Take Note

Salt-n-Pepa spice up #9. This all-female group opened the door for women in hip hop. The group's confident and sassy approach also altered how women in hip hop were portrayed. Salt-n-Pepa's huge crossover hits helped hip hop reach a wider audience.
- Both Salt and Pepa say that motherhood changed the way they perform. How would parenthood affect a celebrity?

SALT N PEPA SHOW

5   4   3   2   1

(8) LAURYN HILL

In 1998, Lauryn Hill was nominated for 10 Grammy Awards for her debut album The Miseducation of Lauryn Hill. She won five — setting a record at the time for most Grammy Awards ever won by a female artist.

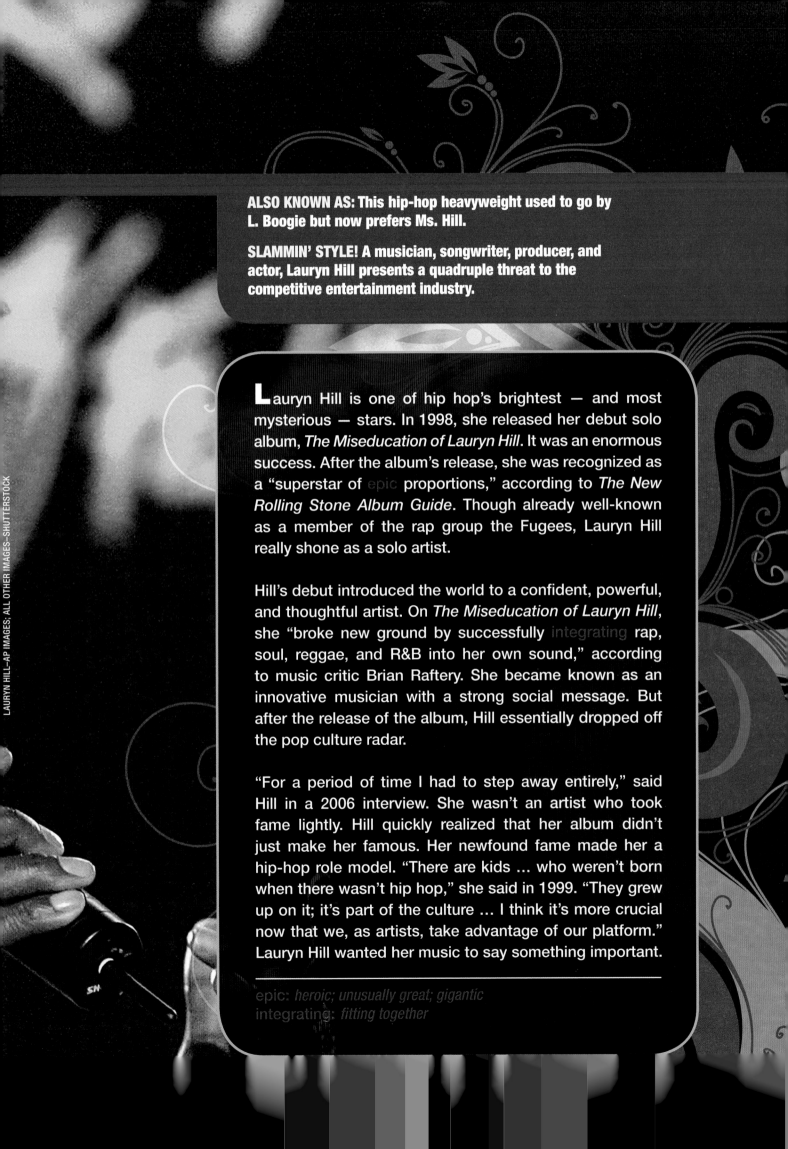

ALSO KNOWN AS: This hip-hop heavyweight used to go by L. Boogie but now prefers Ms. Hill.

SLAMMIN' STYLE! A musician, songwriter, producer, and actor, Lauryn Hill presents a quadruple threat to the competitive entertainment industry.

Lauryn Hill is one of hip hop's brightest — and most mysterious — stars. In 1998, she released her debut solo album, *The Miseducation of Lauryn Hill*. It was an enormous success. After the album's release, she was recognized as a "superstar of epic proportions," according to *The New Rolling Stone Album Guide*. Though already well-known as a member of the rap group the Fugees, Lauryn Hill really shone as a solo artist.

Hill's debut introduced the world to a confident, powerful, and thoughtful artist. On *The Miseducation of Lauryn Hill*, she "broke new ground by successfully integrating rap, soul, reggae, and R&B into her own sound," according to music critic Brian Raftery. She became known as an innovative musician with a strong social message. But after the release of the album, Hill essentially dropped off the pop culture radar.

"For a period of time I had to step away entirely," said Hill in a 2006 interview. She wasn't an artist who took fame lightly. Hill quickly realized that her album didn't just make her famous. Her newfound fame made her a hip-hop role model. "There are kids … who weren't born when there wasn't hip hop," she said in 1999. "They grew up on it; it's part of the culture … I think it's more crucial now that we, as artists, take advantage of our platform." Lauryn Hill wanted her music to say something important.

---

epic: *heroic; unusually great; gigantic*
integrating: *fitting together*

LAURYN HILL

EARLY DAYS

Lauryn Hill was born in South Orange, New Jersey. In the late '80s, she joined forces with Prakazrel "Pras" Michel and Wyclef Jean to form the rap group the Fugees. In 1996, the Fugees released *The Score*. The album "marked the beginning of a resurgence in alternative hip hop," according to music critic Steve Huey. In alternative hip hop, artists blend genres. They incorporate everything from blues and jazz to reggae and pop into a hip-hop sound. *The Score's* popularity inspired Lauryn Hill to make a solo album.

---

resurgence: *rebirth; comeback*

Lauryn Hill shows off her five Grammy Awards in 1998.

BIG BREAK

After the success of *The Score,* Hill created a solo album so she could control every part of the creative process. On the album, Hill explored issues of individuality, feminism, love, and spirituality. She rapped about the individual's place in society and the dangers of relying on money, fame, or image for happiness. On the song "Everything is Everything," Hill explained that she "wrote these words for everyone/Who struggles in their youth/Who won't accept deception/Instead of what is truth." By using the word "miseducation" in her album's title, Hill showed how she herself had been misled in the past by false values. *The Miseducation of Lauryn Hill* also "managed to filter hip hop through a womanist lens," according to *The New Rolling Stone Album Guide*. The album appealed to women who saw Hill as a strong, confident role model.

AT THE TOP

The Miseducation of Lauryn Hill expertly moved "from rapping to singing, from hip hop to neosoul, from African-American [slang] to Jamaican patois," according to *TIME* magazine music critic Christopher John Farley. Clever wordplay and meaningful lyrics appealed to a wide audience. Hill's "rhymes are often about her capabilities, her confidence and what she expects from the world," wrote Jon Pareles in the *New York Times*. At the same time, Hill isn't afraid to "admit to heartache and vulnerability." With her debut, Lauryn Hill redefined hip hop for the '90s.

---

womanist: *believing in and respecting the abilities and talents of women*
neosoul: *modern variety of soul music; mix of jazz and funk*
patois: *language formed from a combination of other languages; Jamaican patois is based on African languages as well as English, Spanish, Portuguese, and Hindi*

? In 2006, Lauryn Hill told an interviewer that one of her hopes for today's artists "is that they don't get trapped in images that don't really reflect who they are." What does she mean by this? Do you think artists sometimes get lost behind public images that have little to do with their real personalities? Explain.

8   7   6

Thats Ms ★ Hill to You!

Because of her range of talent, it was a huge shock when Lauryn Hill turned her back on fame. However, her legacy as one of the most influential hip-hop artists of all time can't be erased. She refused to compromise herself for fame. Read these quotes from Ms. Hill herself and from those around her and see whether you understand her decision.

"I'm Ms. Hill because I know I'm a wise woman. That is the respect I deserve."

— Lauryn Hill

"When you're constantly giving huge chunks of yourself as Lauryn was, sometimes you have to do things that seem eccentric or crazy to maintain your own sanity."

— Talib Kweli, rapper

"I had created this public persona, this public illusion, and it held me hostage. I couldn't be a real person, because [I was] too afraid of what [the] public [would] say ..."

— Lauryn Hill

"The doors were open for Hill to create a multimedia empire of the sort that J.Lo ... [has] built. ... Hill could have been J.Lo with political substance."

— Touré, Rolling Stone magazine

"It just so happens that she's done something that captured a moment in people's lives. They want more ... but she's not ready to give that."

— Prakazrel "Pras" Michel

Quick Fact

In 1999, *Ebony* magazine named Lauryn Hill one of the 100 Most Influential Black Americans. At 23, Hill was the youngest woman ever included on the list.

The Expert Says...

❝ [Lauryn Hill's] rawness, her honesty, her vulnerability about love, her budding moral and spiritual consciousness ... shocked the world into realizing that hip hop could still offer access to a higher plane. ❞

— Joan Morgan, *Essence* magazine

consciousness: self-*awareness*
plane: *level*

Take Note

Musical master Lauryn Hill takes the #8 spot. With her debut album, Hill took hip hop in an entirely new direction. Her songs mixed elements of several genres into a hip-hop hybrid. Hill is considered by many to be hip hop's most influential female artist.

• Most musicians hope that their music will make them into stars. For Lauryn Hill, though, fame was too much to handle. What are the advantages and disadvantages of being famous?

SAXON: ALL OTHER IMAGES: SHUTTERSTOCK

5   4   3   2   1

17

(7) EMINEM

Eminem receives the
award for Best Video of
the Year at the 2002 MTV
Video Music Awards.

ALSO KNOWN AS: Before he was famous, Eminem was known as Marshall Bruce Mathers III.

SLAMMIN' STYLE! Eminem is a Grammy and Oscar winning rapper. He is one of the best-selling rap artists of all time.

It was 1999 when this outspoken artist first told the world, "My name is Slim Shady." People everywhere have been paying attention ever since! The song "My Name Is" was the second single off 1999's *The Slim Shady LP*. This wasn't Eminem's first album, but it was the one that made him a star. *The Slim Shady LP* sold more than three million copies. It also earned Eminem his first of nine Grammy Awards!

The Slim Shady LP made it clear that Eminem wasn't afraid to speak his mind about anything and everything. The album also highlighted the artist's incredible talent. Combining his unique nasal sound with his impressive command of cadence, Eminem delivered an aggressive, catchy, and novel sound. Throughout his career, Eminem's raps have earned him both praise and criticism. Eminem's tough childhood and family issues have inspired much of his work. His various personas, such as Slim Shady, often express prejudiced opinions and display violent tendencies. But Eminem doesn't only write angry lyrics. In many cases, he uses sarcasm to satirize people or issues. Eminem's personas are "a very clever use of literary devices ... a very clever way to try and be a storyteller," according to music critic Nelson George. Part of Eminem's popularity is due to the fact that he expresses "the unspoken things that are going on in this country," according to George.

Since Eminem emerged on the hip-hop scene, he has taken rap in new directions by pushing boundaries and challenging old rules. Eminem is a hugely talented rapper and writer as well as an influential hip-hop artist.

cadence: *flow of sounds when speaking; the beat and rhythm of these sounds*
personas: *characters; roles*
satirize: *expose human shortcomings or foolishness using ridicule or wit*

EMINEM

EARLY DAYS

Eminem never knew his father, and his family moved many times. When he was 11, the family settled in Detroit's tough east side. Eminem was one of few white students in his grade. Small for his age, he was bullied and picked on. But his talent for rhyming didn't go unnoticed. As a teenager, he started competing in local rap battles. He became known as the next "great white hope" in hip-hop circles because earlier white rappers were sometimes considered over-hyped and untalented. In 1997, Eminem released *Infinite*, his first solo CD.

BIG BREAK

Eminem's first solo CD wasn't a success. After its release, he was more determined than ever to make his mark. "I was playin in the beginnin," rapped Eminem in the song "Lose Yourself" in 2002. But, "the mood all changed/I been chewed up and spit out and booed off stage/But I kept rhymin." The artist's persistence eventually paid off. In 1998, he released *The Slim Shady EP*. This album was a "mean-spirited, funny, and thought-provoking record," according to music critic Stephen Erlewine. The album got Eminem noticed by none other than Dr. Dre — one of hip hop's most influential producers! Dr. Dre helped Eminem get a record deal. He also agreed to produce Eminem's next album. The result was 1999's massively popular *The Slim Shady LP*.

> Eminem has been accused of spreading racism, hatred, and sexism through his work. Do you think artists should consider the impact their work might have on other people? Explain.

The Expert Says...

> Eminem ... [flaunts] a style with more verbal muscle and imagination than any of his contemporaries.

— Stephen Erlewine, allmusic.com

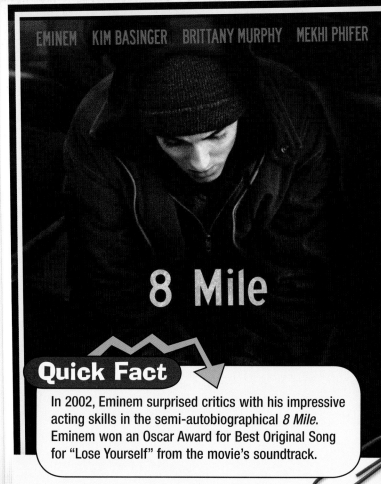

EMINEM   KIM BASINGER   BRITTANY MURPHY   MEKHI PHIFER

8 Mile

Quick Fact

In 2002, Eminem surprised critics with his impressive acting skills in the semi-autobiographical *8 Mile*. Eminem won an Oscar Award for Best Original Song for "Lose Yourself" from the movie's soundtrack.

AT THE TOP

Released in 2000, Eminem's follow-up album was *The Marshall Mathers LP*. It debuted at #1! The album secured Eminem's place as the most successful rapper since Tupac Shakur and Snoop Dogg. Eminem has been so popular, in part, because of his ability to make records that appeal to hip-hop fans as well as to people unfamiliar with the genre. Songs like "My Name Is" and "The Real Slim Shady" were huge crossover hits. Both songs became hits thanks to their catchy sound. Eminem's witty rhymes and fresh approach also appealed to many people. "[Eminem] turned rap in a new direction," according to MTV. He was "constantly pushing boundaries and striking a cord with an ever-widening spectrum of people."

spectrum: *range*

Quick Fact

Eminem has sold more than 70 million albums since his career took off! He is the best-selling music artist of the 21st century so far, according to MTV.

UNLIKELY STAR

An article from CBC News
By Matthew McKinnon
July 26, 2005

[Before Eminem, rap] music was entrenched as the soundtrack of suburbia, but white practitioners of the craft remained the punchline to any number of bad jokes. … Hence the surprise when A-list producer Dr. Dre … stretched his fingers all the way to Michigan to pluck up Marshall Bruce Mathers III, a slight, white MC with a growing reputation for saying vile things into a microphone. …

In the six years since Dre guided him into the mainstream, Marshall Mathers has become one of the planet's most accomplished musicians. He is a nine-time Grammy winner who has sold [more than 70] million albums worldwide, and rewritten the rules of the rap game along the way. … It's a reach to claim he single-handedly integrated rap music. But by proving beyond doubt that pigment does not predict microphone control, Mathers blazed a trail that leads to hip hop's present position. …

Mathers is [35] years old now, as much an adult as he'll ever be. He… is widely accepted on the short list of hip hop's all-time greatest MCs. …

---

entrenched: *firmly established*
A-list: *group of people who are thought to be the most important in their field*
integrated: *opened to all races or ethnic groups*
pigment: *skin color*

? Some people have compared Eminem to Elvis Presley. If you don't know why their careers are similar, find out. In what ways has each one of them influenced the music world?

Take Note

Eminem takes the #7 spot. He is recognized for his one-of-a-kind talent, his genius at writing lyrics, and for his groundbreaking role in hip hop. The popularity of Eminem's albums has helped hip hop become one of the world's best-selling genres.

• Some people think that Eminem uses various personas as a clever way to explore controversial topics. Others think that he hides behind these characters. What do you think? How might the personas Eminem uses affect how people interpret or react to his music?

Quick Fact

According to the *Guinness Book of World Records*, *The Marshall Mathers LP* is the fastest-selling rap album of all time. The album sold more than 1.7 million copies in the U.S. in its first week!

5   4   3   2   1

(6) KANYE WEST

In 2005, TIME magazine named 27-year-old Kanye West one of the World's 100 Most Influential People. "By baring his flaws and being self-critical ... West makes message music you can dance to," wrote Josh Tyrangiel.

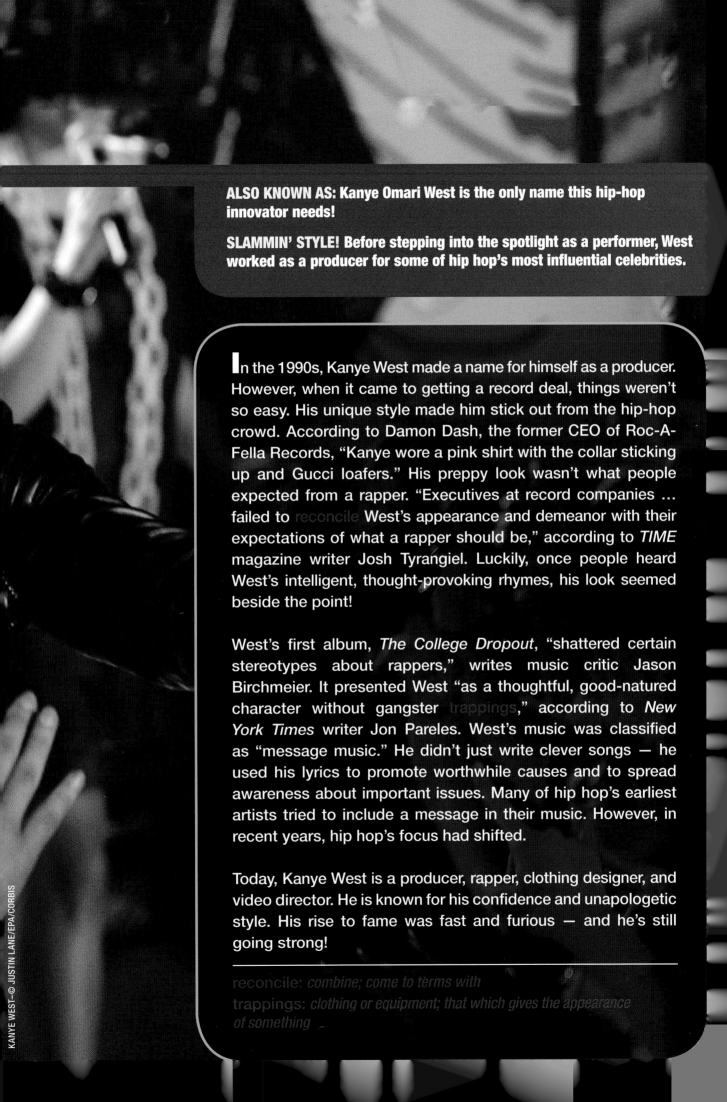

ALSO KNOWN AS: Kanye Omari West is the only name this hip-hop innovator needs!

SLAMMIN' STYLE! Before stepping into the spotlight as a performer, West worked as a producer for some of hip hop's most influential celebrities.

In the 1990s, Kanye West made a name for himself as a producer. However, when it came to getting a record deal, things weren't so easy. His unique style made him stick out from the hip-hop crowd. According to Damon Dash, the former CEO of Roc-A-Fella Records, "Kanye wore a pink shirt with the collar sticking up and Gucci loafers." His preppy look wasn't what people expected from a rapper. "Executives at record companies ... failed to reconcile West's appearance and demeanor with their expectations of what a rapper should be," according to *TIME* magazine writer Josh Tyrangiel. Luckily, once people heard West's intelligent, thought-provoking rhymes, his look seemed beside the point!

West's first album, *The College Dropout*, "shattered certain stereotypes about rappers," writes music critic Jason Birchmeier. It presented West "as a thoughtful, good-natured character without gangster trappings," according to *New York Times* writer Jon Pareles. West's music was classified as "message music." He didn't just write clever songs — he used his lyrics to promote worthwhile causes and to spread awareness about important issues. Many of hip hop's earliest artists tried to include a message in their music. However, in recent years, hip hop's focus had shifted.

Today, Kanye West is a producer, rapper, clothing designer, and video director. He is known for his confidence and unapologetic style. His rise to fame was fast and furious — and he's still going strong!

---

reconcile: *combine; come to terms with*

trappings: *clothing or equipment; that which gives the appearance of something*

KANYE WEST

Quick Fact

In 2007, Kanye West arranged for his third album, *Graduation*, to be released on the same day as *Curtis* — an album by his hip-hop rival 50 Cent. In their first week on the shelves, West's album outsold 50 Cent's by 266,000 copies!

EARLY DAYS

Kanye West was born in 1977 in Atlanta, Georgia. His parents divorced when he was three. West and his mother, a university professor, then moved to Chicago. As a teenager, West discovered his interest in hip hop. After one year of college, he switched his focus to producing rap records. "Within a few months he had his first major sale — $8,000 from a Chicago rapper named Gravity," according to writer Josh Tyrangiel. West also produced several songs on what many think is Jay-Z's best album, 2001's *The Blueprint*.

BIG BREAK

As a producer, West made creative use of vintage R&B records and live instruments. But his biggest break came as a performer. In 2004, West released *The College Dropout*. On the album, he created a signature sound involving soul and gospel music. The album's first single was "Through the Wire." The song was about a 2002 car accident that almost killed him. In 2005, Darryl McDaniels of Run-DMC said, "This past decade it seems like hip hop has mostly been about parties and guns and women." West's album offered something new. It introduced a new sound to hip hop. It also proved that a rapper could tackle serious issues and still be popular.

---

vintage: *classic; old*

> What does Kanye West's unique style say about the evolution of hip hop? Why is it important that someone like West has become famous?

AT THE TOP

West followed his first success with the release of 2005's *Late Registration*. The album sold close to 900,000 copies in its first week! The album also won three Grammy Awards, including the prize for Best Rap Album. In 2004, West founded his own record label, Getting Out Our Dreams (aka G.O.O.D. Music), which has represented artists such as John Legend and Common. Throughout his career, both as a musician and a producer for other artists, West has continued to promote message music. West has tried to reconnect with hip hop's roots. He has promoted hip hop as a genre that can educate and enlighten as well as entertain.

> In the song "Diamonds from Sierra Leone," West tries to educate listeners about the evils of the diamond trade. Many of his works discuss important social issues. Why do you think famous musicians can have an impact with what they say?

Kanye West performs in October 2007.

The Expert Says...

" What's so great about Kanye is that he doesn't fit into the hip-hop/R&B landscape, as we've known it ... he's expanding hip hop lyrically by being more topical. "

— Quddus Phillippe, former MTV VJ

topical: *dealing with matters of current interest*

Quick Fact

While recovering from his 2002 car accident, West heard the Chaka Khan song "Through the Fire." It inspired him to write "Through the Wire," which he recorded even though his jaw was broken and wired shut!

One of a Kind!

Kanye West has his family and his natural talent to thank for an amazing career. Find out more about both in this article.

Growing up with two important role models in his life, Kanye West was in a position to change the course of hip-hop history! West's father, Ray, was a Black Panther. Formed in the late 1960s, the Black Panther Party was a radical political organization that promoted civil rights for African Americans. The party encouraged the use of violence as a means to achieve equality. Donda, Kanye's mother, was a college professor who taught English. West's parents made him politically aware. They also taught him the importance of literacy. Thanks to their influence, Kanye West has been able to craft unique, socially-conscious rhymes.

West's parents had a big influence on him. But you've got to give credit where credit's due! Kanye West's natural talent and skills as a producer allowed him to become an innovative hip-hop artist. West's interest in various musical genres, from Motown to jazz and R&B, helped him infuse hip hop with a novel sound. The focus he put on political and social issues in his lyrics also brought something new to hip hop. From the beginning, West made it clear that he wasn't interested in what other hip-hop artists were saying, wearing, or doing. His one-of-a-kind approach helped redefine hip hop for the new millenium.

West was close to his mother, Donda, who died suddenly in November 2007. A week after her death, he broke into tears during a live performance of "Hey Mama" — the crowd gave him a three-minute standing ovation.

In 2006, West told *Rolling Stone* magazine that he wanted to "have some sort of influence on the culture and to change the sound of music." Looks like he can check this goal off his list! West says that his accomplishments have allowed him to "inspire up-and-coming artists to go against the grain." This influential hip-hop artist is just starting to make his mark.

---

radical: *extreme; promoting drastic reform*

Kanye West's mom was a college professor. His father was a photojournalist and civil rights activist. In what ways do you think West's parents influenced his career and his music?

Take Note

Kanye West's hits produce a #6 ranking! West has influenced hip hop from behind the scenes and from in front of the microphone. He made it clear that hip hop had more than one look. He also crafted timely, inspiring rhymes that spoke to people everywhere. Through his success, West has re-popularized message music and helped bring hip hop back to its roots.

- Kanye West is all about spreading awareness through his music. Do you think musicians can really educate or influence people through their music? Make a list of songs that have made a difference thanks to their message. What did each one teach?

In 2001, *The Source* magazine named the Notorious B.I.G. the greatest rapper of all time. In 2006, MTV ranked him #3 on its list of the Greatest MCs of All Time.

US B.I.G.

NOTORIOUS B.I.G.—AP PHOTO/MARK LENNIHAN, FILE

ALSO KNOWN AS: Born Christopher Wallace, this robust rapper went by the names Biggie Smalls, Big Poppa, Frank White, and the Notorious B.I.G.

SLAMMIN' STYLE! Biggie made a huge impact on hip hop even though he only recorded two albums before his death.

In 1997, at the age of 24, the Notorious B.I.G. became a rap martyr. A talented, up-and-coming artist, Biggie released only one album before he was shot to death in Los Angeles. Biggie grew up in the inner city. He had firsthand experience of the dangers associated with gang violence and drugs. As a young man, though, it looked as though Biggie's life was turning around. He had started to impress people with his witty, impressive rhymes and his talent for delivering them.

Biggie made such a mark on hip hop that he was credited with reviving East Coast rap. When Biggie came onto the scene, East Coast rap was still known for its focus on rhyming technique. West Coast rap, which emphasized storytelling and beats, was more popular. "Biggie re-established East Coast rap's viability," according to music critic Steve Huey. Biggie was an exceptional storyteller. He had a wealth of experiences to draw on for his rhymes. Instead of glorifying street life the way other rappers of the day often did, Biggie gave listeners a realistic and often sad glimpse into what it was really like.

Biggie combined a natural talent for writing, a distinctive, husky voice, and an awareness of street culture into something unique. As hip-hop pioneer Kurtis Blow once said, "[Biggie's] lyrics were really hardcore, expressing his innermost feelings coming from a Brooklyn ghetto. And he was real, because everything he said, he lived that life." His life may have ended prematurely, but Biggie's music has endured and is still influencing hip hop today.

martyr: *someone who reaches great fame through death*
viability: *chance of succeeding or gaining popularity*
hardcore: *realistic in a harsh way*

THE NOTORIOUS B.I.G.

The Notorious B.I.G. in a picture from 1997 taken shortly before his death

EARLY DAYS

Born and raised in Brooklyn, New York, Biggie was an only child. When Biggie was two years old, his father left the family. Biggie's mother worked two jobs to make ends meet. From a young age, Biggie was interested in rapping. With a knack for entertaining people and describing things in a captivating way, he was asked to perform with several local groups. At 17, Biggie dropped out of school. Over the next couple of years, he got a firsthand taste of the criminal lifestyle that inspired his famous songs. Biggie's lyrics often described violent events and people with violent personalities. But Biggie's work didn't glorify violence. Many critics feel that Biggie himself felt trapped by violence and saw it as something that oppresses people instead of giving them freedom.

? Biggie was a good student. He won several English prizes in elementary school. How might Biggie's early education have influenced his songwriting later in life?

BIG BREAK

In 1991, Biggie made a demo tape under the name Biggie Smalls. Mister Cee, a New York-based DJ, promoted the demo on the radio. In 1992, Biggie was featured in *The Source* magazine's "Unsigned Hype" column. It wasn't long before record company executives were taking the time to listen to Biggie's tape! "I got that venom rhyme like Sprite got lemon-lime/Donna Karan dime, keep her hair done all the time," from the song "Realms of Junior M.A.F.I.A." is a good example of what caught the attention of record producers. Biggie had a unique talent. His lyrics rhymed and sounded smooth but also had a message. In 1993, Biggie signed with Bad Boy Records. A year later, he released his first album, *Ready to Die*.

? Biggie was lucky that his first demo tape got such a good reception! What are some ways that artists can get noticed when they're new on the music scene?

AT THE TOP

As 1995 drew to a close, Biggie was the top-selling male solo artist on both the U.S. pop and R&B charts. His success "paved the way to popular success for other East Coast talents like Jay-Z and Nas," according to Steve Huey. As his fame was increasing, though, Biggie was also in the middle of an East Coast vs. West Coast feud with rapper Tupac Shakur. In 1994, Shakur was shot and badly injured outside Quad Recording Studios in New York City. Shakur believed that Biggie and his producer Sean Combs were responsible for the shooting. In 1996, Shakur was murdered in Las Vegas. After his death, Biggie became concerned for his own safety. On March 9, 1997, Biggie was killed in Los Angeles, California.

Quick Fact

Biggie's second album, *Life After Death*, was released just three weeks after his death. The album reached #1 on the Billboard charts.

The Expert Says...

" Dudes had to really go hard in the studio to compete at what he did effortlessly. ... [Biggie's *Life After Death* album] set a higher standard in the game forever. "

— The Game, rapper

LIFE After Death

Learn more about Biggie's legacy in this report.

Death didn't spell the absolute end for Biggie. Since he died, he has sold millions of albums. He has also been the subject of many books, films, and articles. Thanks to his impressive role in hip hop, Biggie has also been the recipient of many posthumous awards. Most people in the music world believe that when Biggie died, he had only just begun to reach his potential.

People have continued to honor Biggie because of his substantial impact on hip hop. Patrick Douthit, aka 9th Wonder, is a producer turned faculty artist-in-residence at North Carolina Central University. He teaches a course on the history of hip hop. The class covers the time period between 1978 and March 9, 1997. Douthit believes hip hop changed forever the day Biggie was killed.

"Biggie was the master of style, narrative, and cynical reflection," wrote author Cheo Hodari Coker in his book *Unbelievable: The Life, Death and Afterlife of The Notorious B.I.G.* Biggie wrote "records and songs that could change the way people think about life."

Biggie died prematurely. However, his debut album is considered "one of the greatest hardcore rap albums ever recorded," according to music critic Steve Huey.

---

posthumous: *occurring after one's death*
cynical: *seeing a dark truth beneath what first seems harmless*

Quick Fact

Ready to Die was ranked #133 on *Rolling Stone* magazine's list of the 500 Greatest Albums of All Time. Biggie "took all [his] gritty life experience and crammed it into *Ready to Die*," according to the magazine.

? Three Biggie albums were released posthumously using vocals he recorded during his lifetime. Do you think it's okay to use an artist's vocals in songs he or she never had a chance to hear? How might this affect an artist's reputation? Explain.

A mural in the Bronx, New York, painted in memory of the Notorious B.I.G.

Take Note

The Notorious B.I.G. takes the #5 spot. With his debut album, Biggie caught the hip-hop world's attention. He brought East Coast rap to the front of the hip-hop scene. In his music, Biggie rapped about the dangers of a criminal lifestyle. Rather than glorify it, Biggie emphasized the negative impact of violence. Many believe his premature death stunted hip hop. Though other rappers have copied Biggie's violent imagery, few have been able to show criminality's damaging effects as well as Biggie did.

• Biggie and Tupac Shakur were music rivals. Name some other rivals in the music business. How can rivalry help music evolve? How can it be harmful?

④ TUPAC SHAKUR

In 2007, Tupac Shakur came in at #8 on Forbes magazine's list of top-earning dead celebrities. Shakur's estate continues to earn money thanks to the artist's albums, clothing line, movies, books, and even a Broadway musical.

ALSO KNOWN AS: Shakur used the name 2Pac on most of his records.

SLAMMIN' STYLE! Considered by many to be the greatest rapper of all time, Shakur created a massive body of work in his tragically short life.

Tupac Amaru Shakur lived a life of contradictions. On the one hand, he attended an arts school where he excelled at his studies. At 12, he made his acting debut — landing a role in a play called *A Raisin in the Sun*. He was well-read and creative. He started making a name for himself with well-written poetry and raps. However, the flip side to Shakur's creative genius was the life he rapped about in his songs. When he was 17, Shakur left school. He moved with his family to Marin County, California, where he became involved in crime, violence, and eventually, professional hip hop.

It didn't take long for Shakur to find his way to the top of the rap realm. By 1991, he had a record deal, a popular debut album, and some important ties to the hip-hop community. Soon, people everywhere were noticing Shakur's talent for poetry, music, and acting.

It's no surprise that Shakur is listed in the *Guinness Book of World Records* as the best-selling hip-hop artist of all time. His combination of talents helped him create some of hip hop's most important albums. Tragically, Shakur was shot on September 7, 1996. He died six days later at the age of 25. Despite his death, Shakur's legacy continues even today.

TUPAC SHAKUR

Janet Jackson and Tupac Shakur starred together in the 1993 movie Poetic Justice.

EARLY DAYS

Born in East Harlem in 1971, Shakur was the son of two members of the Black Panther Party. His parents separated before he was born, and Shakur was raised by his mother. He spent his early years in the Bronx and Harlem. The rest of his childhood was unsettled as the family moved around the country. A couple of years after moving to California, Shakur got his foot in the hip-hop door when he was hired as a dancer and roadie by the rap group Digital Underground. He made his debut on the group's 1991 album, *This Is an EP Release*.

Quick Fact

He wrote tough, aggressive lyrics but Shakur could also write emotional, raw poetry. In 2000, *The Rose That Grew From Concrete* was published. Shakur wrote this book of poems when he was just 19 years old.

BIG BREAK

In 1992, Shakur released his first solo album, *2Pacalypse Now*. This album dealt with the problems facing young African-American males. The album was "significantly more political than the rapper's subsequent releases," according to writer Marisa Brown. Many criticized Shakur for his graphic language and portrayal of violence. Despite the controversy, Shakur had a hit on his hands. The album went gold — selling more than 500,000 copies.

subsequent: *following*

Quick Fact

Shakur's debut album, *2Pacalypse Now*, generated a lot of controversy when it was released. Then Vice President Dan Quayle criticized the album saying, "It has no place in our society."

Is there a connection between poetry and song lyrics? How might writing poetry help musicians express themselves in song? In what ways is writing poetry different than writing a novel or story?

AT THE TOP

After the success of his debut, Shakur was in high demand. He resurrected his acting career with roles in the movies *Juice*, *Poetic Justice*, and *Above the Rim*. Despite his success, Shakur started having a lot of trouble with the law. He was in jail when his album *Me Against the World,* which entered the charts at #1, was released. Around this time, the now-infamous West Coast vs. East Coast feud was intensifying. On September 13, 1996, Tupac Shakur died after being hit four times in a drive-by shooting in Las Vegas.

infamous: *scandalous; notorious*

Dan Quayle wanted Shakur's album to be censored because of its graphic and controversial content. Do you think censorship goes against freedom of speech? Do you think censorship is a good or a bad thing? Explain.

The Many Sides of Tupac

Most people recognize Tupac Shakur as a rapper whose all-too-real criminal lifestyle caught up with him. But there were many sides to this artist. Movie critic Mark Deming once said that Shakur was both "a hard-edged gangster rapper, and a poet who wrote with sensitivity and concern about life in the African-American community." Take a look at this chart and discover the many sides of Tupac Shakur.

ON THE ONE HAND ...

Shakur dropped out of high school when he was 17. He lived on the streets and sold drugs.

When his music career started taking off, he became involved in several violent crimes.

Several of his songs fit the gangster-rap genre — they're filled with graphic lyrics and express violent, aggressive emotions.

Tupac Shakur was a convicted felon.

ON THE OTHER ...

Before dropping out, Shakur excelled at a prestigious arts high school.

Shakur was insightful and aware. These characteristics helped him in his acting. He could portray life on the streets with compassion and insight.

Shakur was a sensitive poet. According to author Soren Baker, in his lyrics he "tackled ... personal, timeless issues." In his writings, Shakur showed his sensitive nature. He wrote about everything from love and passion to disappointment and his own insecurities.

Shakur was a social activist. In his music, he highlighted many of the problems facing America's youth. He fought for governments to address these issues.

? When the rapper Nas was starting out, he was part of the violent, dangerous street life that he rapped about in his songs. Today, he is considered a wise and insightful artist. Do you think hip hop would be in a healthier state right now if Tupac Shakur had lived and had a chance to grow as an artist? Explain.

The Expert Says...

" Every rapper who grew up in the '90s owes something to Tupac. ... He didn't sound like anyone who came before him. "

— 50 Cent, rapper

Take Note

Tupac Shakur is our pick for #4. Shot at the age of 25, he came to symbolize the violence he rapped about in his songs. Shakur has reached iconic status in the hip-hop world. His many albums and movies continue to inspire musicians and fans.

• Shakur once said, "I loved going to school. It taught me a lot. I was starting to feel like I really wanted to be an artist." What classes do you think helped Shakur most in his career? How might higher education have influenced his life and art?

③ RUN-DMC

From left to right, Joseph Simmons, Jason Mizell, and Darryl McDaniels

ALSO KNOWN AS: Run-DMC was made up of Joseph "Reverend Run" Simmons, Jason "Jam Master Jay" Mizell, and Darryl "DMC" McDaniels.

SLAMMIN' STYLE! Run-DMC was the first rap group to have a music video played on MTV. The group's debut album was the first rap album to go gold by selling more than 500,000 copies!

They may not have been the first group to make it big in hip hop, but Run-DMC truly brought hip hop to the masses. In the late 1970s and early '80s, both Grandmaster Flash and the Sugarhill Gang had hip-hop hits. However, they were considered just part of a fad. Run-DMC was the first group to prove that hip hop was going to be around for a long time. The group helped define hip-hop's sound. With their hats, gold chains, and untied sneakers, the members of the group also helped define the look of hip hop. As Chuck D of Public Enemy said in 2004, "Run-DMC dressed … like cats off the street — and 20 years later, most rappers still dress the same way."

Run-DMC also meshed genres in an innovative way. By crossing over into hard rock, the group widened its audience base beyond pure rap fans. "The trio helped change the course of popular music, paving the way for rap's second generation," according to *The Rolling Stone Encyclopedia of Rock and Roll*.

Run-DMC popularized rap and made people around the world more open to the hip-hop sound. As written in *The Rolling Stone Encyclopedia of Rock and Roll*, "Run-DMC took hardcore hip hop from an underground street sensation to a pop-culture phenomenon."

cats: *slang word to describe cool people*

RUN-DMC

? Who do you think has had a greater influence on hip hop — Russell Simmons or Run-DMC? Why?

EARLY DAYS

The three members of Run-DMC grew up in Hollis, Queens, in New York City. In the early 1980s, Joseph Simmons's older brother Russell thought it would be a good idea for Joseph to form a rap duo with Darryl McDaniels. Russell was co-founder of a hip-hop management company called Rush Productions. With Russell Simmons in their corner, Run and DMC started rapping together. Jam Master Jay joined as their DJ after their graduation from high school.

Quick Fact

Russell Simmons was the mastermind behind Run-DMC, but he didn't stop there! Simmons is one of hip hop's greatest entrepreneurs. His label, Def Jam Records, represents everyone from Rihanna to Nas! He's also the founder of the Phat Farm fashion label.

BIG BREAK

In 1983, Run-DMC released its first single. "It's Like That" was a hip-hop novelty. "The single sounded like no other rap at the time," according to music critic Stephen Erlewine. It was grittier and harder than everything that had come before. Run-DMC became known as the first hardcore rap group. The group rapped about its troubles and about problems in the inner city. The group's sound was also more aggressive than earlier hip hop. Run-DMC focused on beats not catchy tunes. ["It's Like That"] was the first 'new school' hip-hop recording," according to Erlewine. The song became a top 20 R&B hit! In 1985, the group released *King of Rock*, its second album. The album established the group as "the most popular and influential rappers in America," writes Erlewine. On the album, Run-DMC broke "down the barriers between rock and roll and rap."

AT THE TOP

In 1986, Run-DMC joined forces with rock legends Steven Tyler and Joe Perry of Aerosmith. Together, the musicians recorded a cover of Aerosmith's "Walk This Way." The song appealed to both rockers and rappers. It peaked at #4 on the pop charts and #1 on the R&B charts! According to *TIME* magazine writer Josh Tyrangiel, "[The collaboration was] rap's first masterpiece." This classic cemented Run-DMC's place in hip-hop history. As Chuck D of Public Enemy once said, "Jay-Z, OutKast, Black Star, the Roots — everyone in hip hop today can be traced back to Run-DMC."

? Run-DMC and Aerosmith worked together to create the hit single, "Walk This Way." Name other songs that successfully combined musical genres and styles. What made them work?

In 2002, Jam Master Jay was murdered. In an interview that year, Run stated, "No one will want to see Run-DMC without Jam Master Jay. Run-DMC is officially retired."

RUN-DMC
ROCKING THE WORLD!

The members of Run-DMC changed the course of music forever. Read this list to fully understand the group's impact.

1. PIONEERS

- The members of Run-DMC were the first rappers to appear on the cover of *Rolling Stone* magazine.
- Run-DMC was the first rap act to have gold, platinum, and multi-platinum albums.
- The members of Run-DMC were the first rappers to receive a Grammy nomination.
- Thanks to their song "My Adidas," Run-DMC was the first rap act signed to an athletic product endorsement deal.

2. CROSSING GENRES

- The group's cover of "Walk This Way" with Aerosmith helped bring hip hop to the mainstream. The song mixed a classic rock and roll sound with hip-hop elements like rapping and a heavy beat. Heavy rotation of the video on MTV helped increase interest in the song.
- They didn't stop at Aerosmith. The members of Run-DMC have also worked with rockers Everlast, Fred Durst, Kid Rock, and Sugar Ray.

3. TRENDSETTING

- According to rapper and actor Ice-T, "Until Run-DMC I thought that hip hop was something that was only going to be done in basements and in clubs. … [Run-DMC] made me believe that hip hop could be big."
- Eminem once said, "Run-DMC broke down the barriers. They were the first real rap stars. Everyone in the game today owes something to them."

Quick Fact

In 2004, *Rolling Stone* magazine ranked Run-DMC #48 on its list of the 100 Greatest Artists of All Time. The group's crossover hit "Walk This Way" came in at #287 on the magazine's list of the 500 Greatest Songs.

The Expert Says…

" Run-DMC were the Beatles of hip hop. … [Their third album] was the first true rap album, a complete work of art as opposed to a collection of singles or a novelty item. "

— Chuck D, Public Enemy

Take Note

Run-DMC run away with #3! This group pioneered modern hip hop with its style and novel sound. Since the members of the group weren't the fastest or smoothest of rappers, they don't rank higher.

- Many modern hip-hop stars credit Run-DMC with paving the way for their success. How might today's music scene be different if hip hop had never caught on?

2 NAS

When Nas was born, his parents must have known he'd be famous. Nasir is an Arabic name that means "helper" and "victory." Nas has not only helped hip hop evolve, he has triumphed as one of hip hop's most important personalities. Along the way, this star has evolved "from a young street disciple to a vain all-knowing sage to a humbled godly teacher," according to music critic Jason Birchmeier. Early in his career, Nas got people's attention by increasing awareness about conditions in the inner city. His influence grew as he began to focus on the real meaning of life.

It was 1994 when Nas's debut solo CD hit store shelves. *Illmatic* was immediately called "a rap classic" by critics, including *TIME* magazine's Christopher John Farley. The album was "lean, smart, and at times jazzy." Nas's debut "sold very well, spawned multiple hits, and earned unanimous acclaim," writes Jason Birchmeier. Today, Nas's first album is considered one of the greatest hip-hop albums of all time. You might think it would be hard to live up to expectations after such a stellar debut. But Nas has proven that he's up to the task. He's made more than 10 albums — each one containing important, popular, and influential rhymes.

"Despite his years in the game, Nas is still a diamond in the rough," writes Kris Ex in *Rolling Stone* magazine. According to Ex, Nas is "perhaps the rawest lyrical talent of his day."

---

sage: *scholar; intellectual*
unanimous: *of one mind; in complete agreement*
diamond in the rough: *expression describing a talented person who lacks training or polish*

 What do you think Ex meant when he called Nas "the rawest lyrical talent of his day"? Do you think it's an insult or a compliment to call somebody a raw talent?

ALSO KNOWN AS: Born Nasir Jones, Nas performs under a short form of his name.

SLAMMIN' STYLE! From the time he released *Illmatic* in 1994, Nas has been recognized as a hip-hop superstar with something important to say.

Rapper Nas performs in December 2006.

NAS

EARLY DAYS

Nasir Jones was born in 1973 in Long Island City, a neighborhood in New York City. His father, Olu Dara, is a well-known jazz musician. When Nas was very young, he moved with his family to the nearby Queensbridge Houses, a large public housing project. After a few years there, Dara left his family. Nas's mother was left to raise her sons alone. When he was in 9th grade, Nas dropped out of school. He "delved into street culture and flirted with danger, such experiences … characterizing his rhymes," according to writer Birchmeier.

BIG BREAK

In 1991, Nas collaborated with underground artist Main Source on a song called "Live at the Barbeque." Word about his talent spread and Nas was asked to contribute a song to the movie *Zebrahead*. In 1994, Nas released *Illmatic*. His debut lived up to all the anticipation and hype surrounding it. Nas used his first album to condemn the violent lifestyle he saw around him. "Nobody captured the creeping menace of life on the streets like this 20-year-old from New York's Queensbridge projects," according to *Rolling Stone* magazine. On the song "One Time 4 Your Mind," Nas rapped "I'm still writin rhymes but besides that I'm chillin/… cold be starvin make you wanna do crimes kid/But I'm a lamp, cuz a crime couldn't beat a rhyme."

? Like most rappers, Nas uses slang in his lyrics. Do you understand what Nas is rapping about above? If you don't, do some research and find out what these lyrics mean.

The Expert Says…

" [Nas] wants to tell a story, communicate ideas. … [The] ambition of his lyrics and themes is what makes him hip hop's most important and interesting male solo performer. "

— Christopher John Farley, *TIME* magazine

Quick Fact

Like Kanye West, Nas has used his music to raise awareness of social issues. In the song "I Want to Talk to You," Nas rapped "Mr. Mayor imagine if this was your backyard / Mr. Governor imagine if it was your kids that starved." The lyrics urged public officials to do something about the conditions of the inner city.

AT THE TOP

It Was Written, released in 1996, was a bit of a surprise for hardcore hip-hop fans. The album was a crossover success thanks to its pop-friendly tunes. Hip-hop purists accused Nas of selling out but the album was just one step in Nas' development as an artist. As writer Jason Birchmeier points out, Nas has "continually matured as an artist." Trying new things, he has broadened his horizons and made music that appeals to a wide range of listeners.

Quick Fact

Nas's debut, *Illmatic*, was ranked #400 on *Rolling Stone* magazine's list of the 500 Greatest Albums of All Time.

EAST COAST EMPIRE

When hip hop began, it was all East Coast. Get to know a few of history's main players in this East Coast rap flow chart.

DJ KOOL HERC

Herc was the "originator of breakbeat DJing, essentially the essence of hip hop," according to writer Steve Kurutz. Developed in the '70s, Herc's sound influenced everyone — including Kurtis Blow.

RUN-D.M.C.

Joseph Simmons shot to fame as "Run" of Run-DMC. "People can't understand how important [Run-DMC] were in pop music history," according to Jim Tremayne, editor of *DJ Times* magazine.

Joseph Simmons, aka Reverend Run

KURTIS BLOW

Blow was the first rapper to really prove rap could sell. Early on, Blow's DJ was Joseph Simmons.

PUBLIC ENEMY

This group was signed by Def Jam Records — the label co-founded by Joseph Simmons's brother Russell. Public Enemy is recognized for writing revolutionary songs that directly addressed issues affecting the African-American community such as poverty, crime, and racism.

JAY-Z

In 2005, Chuck D of Public Enemy said that "if you had to look in a book for the definition of a rapper you would probably see a picture of Jay-Z."

Kurtis Blow in 1987

NAS

For years, Jay-Z and Nas insulted each other as they fought for the title of king of East Coast rap. "The back-and-forth bout created massive publicity for both," according to Jason Birchmeier. In 2004, both artists decided to put an end to the feud.

Take Note

Nas reigns as our pick for #2. He climbed from the streets to the top of the hip-hop world! His "street cred" helped him appeal to fans of hardcore rap. His collaborations with more mainstream artists helped increase his popularity with fans of other genres. Nas has ruled the hip-hop charts for more than 15 years.

- In 2006, Nas released an album called *Hip Hop Is Dead*. He supposedly chose this controversial title to reflect how hip hop has changed from being a pure art form into being an overly-commercialized business. Do you think hip hop has lost something since its early days? Explain.

breakbeat: *irregular drum pattern, electronically repeated to form a fast rhythm*
bout: *contest*

9

① JAY-Z

Jay-Z's name was inspired by a number of things. As a teen he was known as "Jazzy." When he started rapping he had a mentor whose name was Jaz-O. The J and Z subway lines also stop at Marcy Avenue, near where Jay-Z grew up.

ALSO KNOWN AS: This hip-hop all-star was born Shawn Corey Carter. Apart from Jay-Z, he has also gone by the names Jigga and Jay Hova.

SLAMMIN' STYLE! Jay-Z isn't just a Grammy winning hip-hop artist, he's also a songwriter, record executive, and fashion mogul!

Jay-Z is a hip-hop icon in every sense of the word — enduring and setting trends like no one else in the hip-hop game. Jay-Z grew up in a bleak housing project. Today, he is the wealthiest star in hip hop. And it took a lot more than just mastering a mic to make it this big!

Jay-Z's life story is a classic tale of rags to mega riches. Born in Brooklyn's tough Marcy projects, Jay-Z grew up a world away from the glitzy music industry. As a teenager, though, he started making a name for himself in his neighborhood. Despite his talent, Jay-Z had a hard time getting a recording contract. Instead of giving up, he took matters into his own hands. Since he couldn't land a record deal, Jay-Z created his own label! In 1996, he co-founded Roc-A-Fella Records. That same year, Jay-Z released his debut album, *Reasonable Doubt*, under the Roc-A-Fella label.

Today, Jay-Z is a true business mogul. As an artist, he "has had the courage to tell vivid stories about the realities of the urban experience," according to record executive Russell Simmons. Jay-Z has combined his musical talent with an entrepreneurial spirit. Along the way he's become an enduring hip-hop icon.

---

mogul: *important, powerful, and influential person; big shot*
entrepreneurial: *ambitious about business; enterprising*

JAY-Z

EARLY DAYS

Jay-Z was born in 1969 in Brooklyn, New York. His father left home when he was just 12 years old, and Jay-Z was raised by his mom. She was the one who bought him his first boom box to encourage his interest in music. At that time Jay-Z began freestyling his rhymes (he is famous for being able to write entire songs in his head, never having to write a word on paper). As a teen, Jay-Z turned to the street after dropping out of school. Around this time he met his rap mentor Jaz-O.

freestyling: *making up raps on the spot; improvising*

Quick Fact

In 2007, Jay-Z was ranked the ninth-richest celebrity in the world by *Forbes* magazine. Sean "Diddy" Combs (#43) and 50 Cent (#32) were the only other hip-hop stars on the list.

Jay-Z performs in November 2007

BIG BREAK

Jay-Z's debut, *Reasonable Doubt*, was released in 1996. It "established Jay as the premier freestyle rapper of his generation," according to *Rolling Stone* magazine. On the album, Jay-Z came across as a veteran of the rap scene. "No question; Jay-Z got too many answers/I been around this block, too many times/Rocked, too many rhymes," he rapped on the song "22 Two's." On *Reasonable Doubt*, Jay-Z also detailed "his experiences on the streets with disarming honesty," according to music critic Steve Huey. On the song "Regrets," Jay-Z rapped about his own personal experiences on the street. "In order to survive, gotta learn to live with regrets/On the rise to the top, many drop, don't forget." In 1997, Jay-Z released *In My Lifetime, Vol.1*. With the release of this album, Jay-Z "made his claim for the title of best rapper on the East Coast," according to music critic John Bush.

AT THE TOP

By 2001, with the release of *The Blueprint*, Jay-Z "solidified his position atop the New York rap scene," writes music critic Jason Birchmeier. Despite his popularity, Jay-Z announced his retirement as a performer in 2003. But just three years later, he was back. The release of *Kingdom Come* proved Jay-Z still belonged behind a mic. In 2006, he was named the greatest MC of all time in an MTV survey. "[Jay-Z's] influence is beyond question: If he does it or wears it, chances are his fans and peers will do the same," stated MTV.

What's Jay-Z's advice for how to become a great MC? "[W]rite every day ... because it's like anything else: [You have to] practice," he once said in an interview with MTV. "The more you do it, the better you do." Do you agree with this advice? In what ways might writing make someone a better rapper?

10   9   8   7   6

HIP-HOP HEAVYWEIGHT

Jay-Z has accomplished so many things that it's hard to list them all! But don't just believe the hype — see for yourself in this timeline.

1996 — Together, Jay-Z, Damon Dash, and Kareem "Biggs" Burke found Roc-A-Fella Records.

1996 — Jay-Z releases his first solo album. *Reasonable Doubt* reaches #23 on the Billboard 200. In February 2002, the album reaches platinum status — selling more than one million copies!

1998 — Jay-Z's third album, *Vol. 2. Hard Knock Life,* is released. Later that year, it earns Jay-Z his first Grammy Award for Best Rap Album.

2002 — Up-and-coming artists Cam'ron and Kanye West are signed to Roc-A-Fella Records.

2003 — Jay-Z becomes the first non-athlete to get a signature shoe from a major footwear company. His S. Carter line for Reebok becomes the fastest-selling shoe in the history of the company.

2004 — Executives at Def Jam Records hire Jay-Z to be the company's president and CEO.

2005 — Jay-Z is named one of *TIME* magazine's 100 Most Influential People of the Year. Entrepreneur Russell Simmons writes that "Jay-Z stands center stage with the penetrating sustainability of a living legend."

2007 — In December, Jay-Z steps down from his position as president of Def Jam Records saying, "It's time for me to take on new challenges." A few days later, it is reported that Jay-Z is in talks about starting a record label with the Apple computer company.

sustainability: *strength; longevity*

Take Note

Jay-Z takes #1! Since he burst onto the scene in 1996, his lyrical genius and longevity have allowed him to branch out and impact all aspects of hip-hop culture. He is responsible for some of hip hop's greatest albums — both as an artist and as a producer. After his brief retirement, Jay-Z is back and bigger than ever!

- Do you think Jay-Z's "retirement" might have been a marketing ploy? How might it have affected his popularity? What do you think inspired him to return to the stage?

The Expert Says...

For the last decade Jay-Z has been the world's most reliable rapper, a hitmaker beloved by fans and respected by his peers.

— Kelefa Sanneh, *The New York Times*

We Thought ...

Here are the criteria we used in ranking the 10 most influential hip-hop artists.

The artist:
- Has created innovative music
- Has introduced a new look to hip hop
- Has influenced other musicians
- Has a strong message
- Has been hugely successful
- Has won awards and critical acclaim
- Has carved out a new path
- Has had an impact on all aspects of hip-hop culture
- Has endured

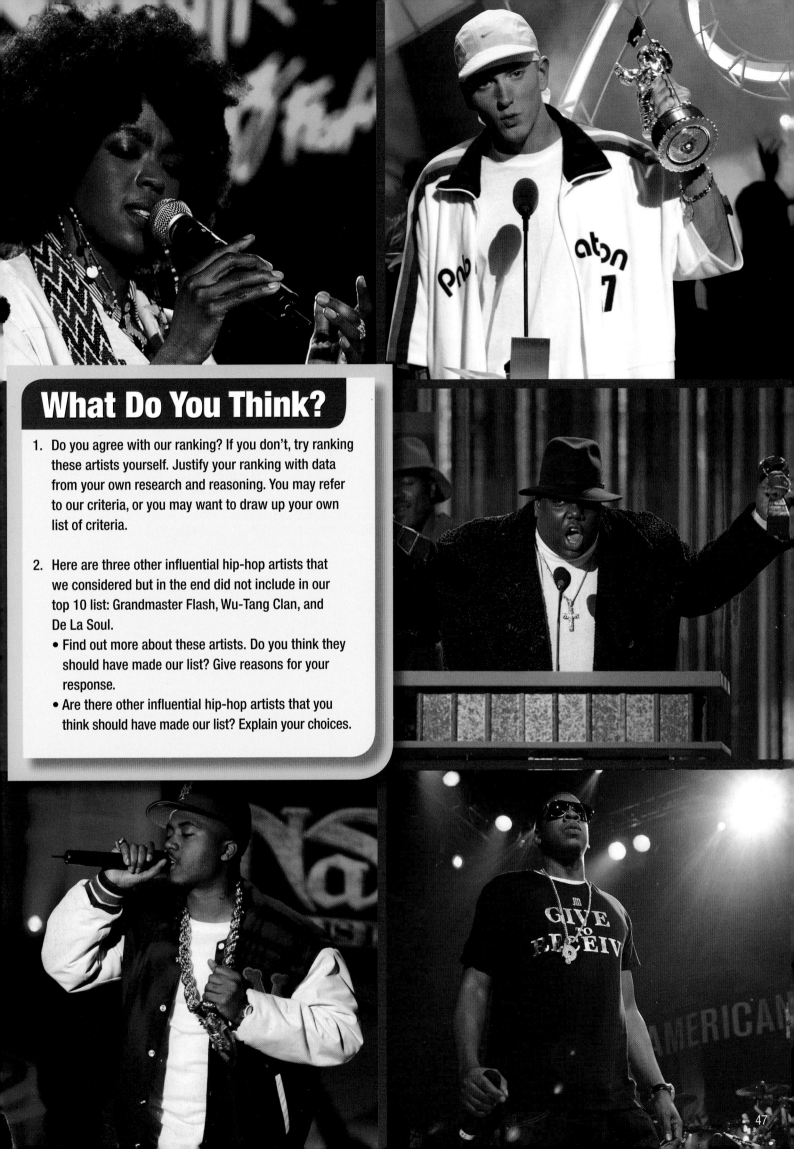

What Do You Think?

1. Do you agree with our ranking? If you don't, try ranking these artists yourself. Justify your ranking with data from your own research and reasoning. You may refer to our criteria, or you may want to draw up your own list of criteria.

2. Here are three other influential hip-hop artists that we considered but in the end did not include in our top 10 list: Grandmaster Flash, Wu-Tang Clan, and De La Soul.
   • Find out more about these artists. Do you think they should have made our list? Give reasons for your response.
   • Are there other influential hip-hop artists that you think should have made our list? Explain your choices.

Index